BIG-NOTE PIANO   3RD EDITION

MODERN MOVIE SONGS

ISBN 978-1-54008-8994

Visit Hal Leonard Online at
www.halleonard.com

Contact us:
Hal Leonard
7777 West Bluemound Road
Milwaukee, WI 53213
Email: info@halleonard.com

In Europe, contact:
Hal Leonard Europe Limited
42 Wigmore Street
Marylebone, London, W1U 2RN
Email: info@halleonardeurope.com

In Australia, contact:
Hal Leonard Australia Pty. Ltd.
4 Lentara Court
Cheltenham, Victoria, 3192 Australia
Email: info@halleonard.com.au

THE BALLAD OF THE LONESOME COWBOY
TOY STORY 4
8

BEAUTIFUL GHOSTS
CATS
3

CRAZY LITTLE THING CALLED LOVE
BOHEMIAN RHAPSODY
12

DOWNTON ABBEY (THEME)
DOWNTON ABBEY
18

ELASTIGIRL IS BACK
INCREDIBLES 2
20

THE HIDDEN WORLD
HOW TO TRAIN YOUR DRAGON: THE HIDDEN WORLD
22

A MILLION DREAMS
THE GREATEST SHOWMAN
24

THE PLACE WHERE LOST THINGS GO
MARY POPPINS RETURNS
32

PROUD CORAZÓN
COCO
36

SHALLOW
A STAR IS BORN
42

SPEECHLESS
ALADDIN
52

SPIRIT
THE LION KING
68

WON'T YOU BE MY NEIGHBOR?
(IT'S A BEAUTIFUL DAY IN THE NEIGHBORHOOD)
A BEAUTIFUL DAY IN THE NEIGHBORHOOD
60

YESTERDAY
YESTERDAY
62

YOUR SONG
ROCKET MAN
64

ZERO
RALPH BREAKS THE INTERNET
47

BEAUTIFUL GHOSTS

from the film CATS

Words and Music by TAYLOR SWIFT
and ANDREW LLOYD WEBBER

Dramatic Ballad

watch from the dark, wait for / my life to start, with no / beau - ty in my mem - o -
call them my friends and be / bro - ken a - gain. Is this / hope just a mys - ti - cal

ry. / dream? All that I want - ed _____

was to be want - ed. _____ { (1., 2.) Too young to
{ (D.S.) I'll nev - er

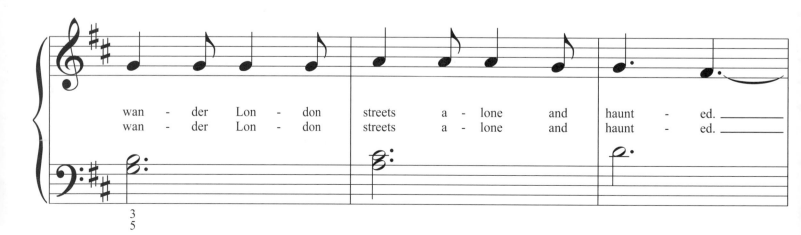

wan - der Lon - don streets a - lone and haunt - ed. _____
wan - der Lon - don streets a - lone and haunt - ed. _____

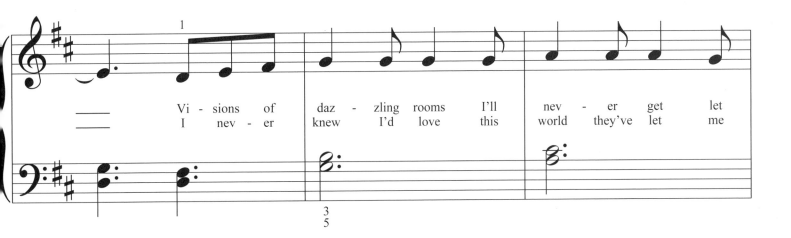

To Coda ⊕

go.
But at least you have beau - ti - ful
go.
So I'll dance with these beau - ti - ful

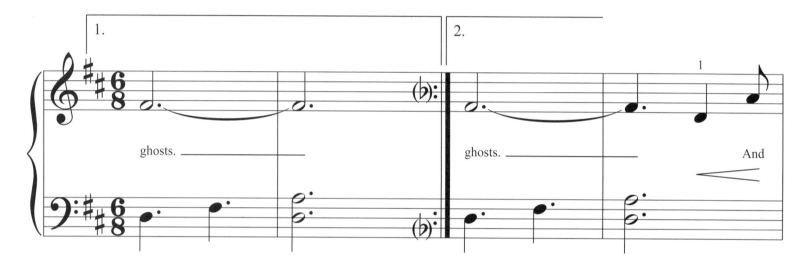

1.
2.

ghosts. _____
ghosts. _____
And

may - be my home is - n't what I had known, what I thought it would be. _____

f

_____ But I feel so a - live with these phan - toms of night. And I

know that this life is-n't safe, but it's wild and it's free. _____

_____ All that I

CODA

ghosts. _____ And the

mem-'ries were lost long a - go, so I'll

dance with these beau-ti-ful ghosts. _____

THE BALLAD OF THE LONESOME COWBOY

from TOY STORY 4

Music and Lyrics by
RANDY NEWMAN

Moderately fast

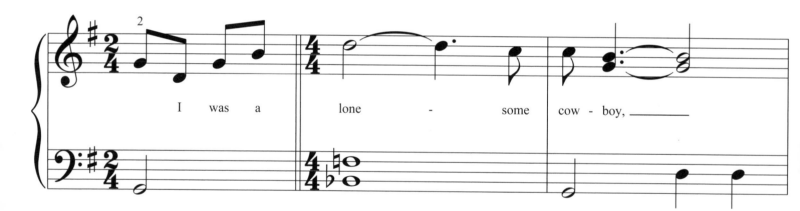

I was a lone - some cow - boy, _____

lone - some as I could be. You came a - long,

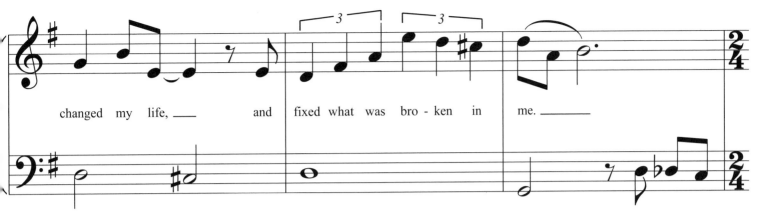

changed my life, ___ and fixed what was bro - ken in me. _____

I was a lone - some cow - boy, _____

I did - n't have a friend. ___ Now I got friends com - in'

out of my ears. ___ I'll nev - er be lone - some a - gain. _____

10

You can't be hap-py when you're all by your-self. Go on, tell me I'm

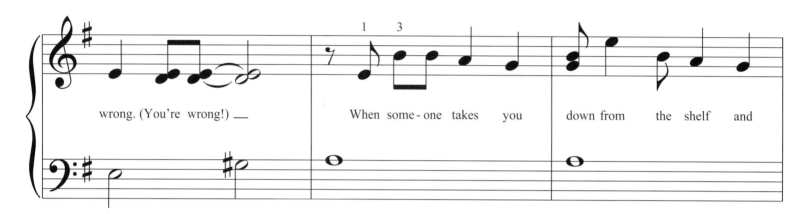

wrong. (You're wrong!) ___ When some-one takes you down from the shelf and

plays with you some, it's won-der-ful. I was a

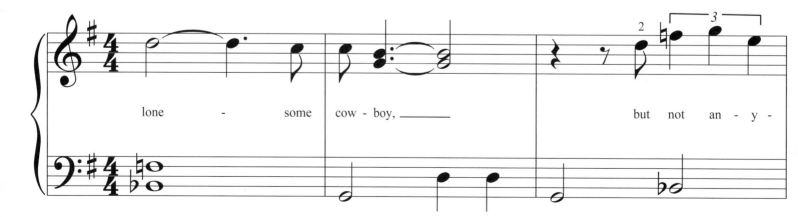

lone - some cow-boy, _____ but not an-y-

more.   I just found out what love is a - bout. ___   I've

nev - er felt this way be - fore. ___   I was a lone - some

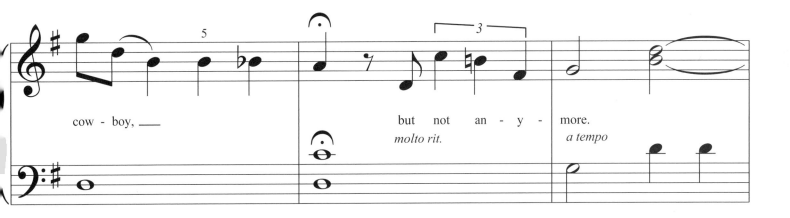

cow - boy, __   but not an - y - more.

molto rit.   *a tempo*

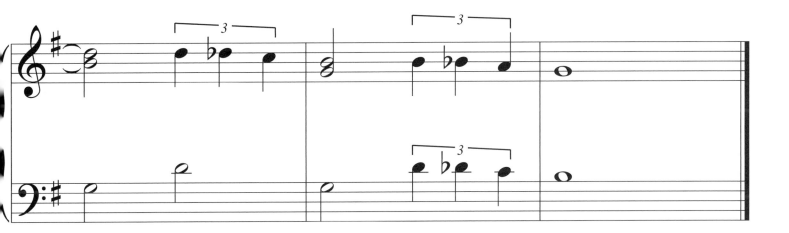

CRAZY LITTLE THING CALLED LOVE

featured in BOHEMIAN RHAPSODY

Words and Music by
FREDDIE MERCURY

13

love.   Well,   this   thing —   There   goes   my

ba   -   by; —   she knows —   how to rock and roll. —

— She drives — me   cra - zy. —   She gives me

hot and cold   fe - ver.   She   leaves me in a cool, cool   sweat.

I got - ta be cool, __

__ re - lax, __ a - get hip, __ a - get

on my tracks. Take a back seat, hitch - hike __ and take a

To Coda ⊕

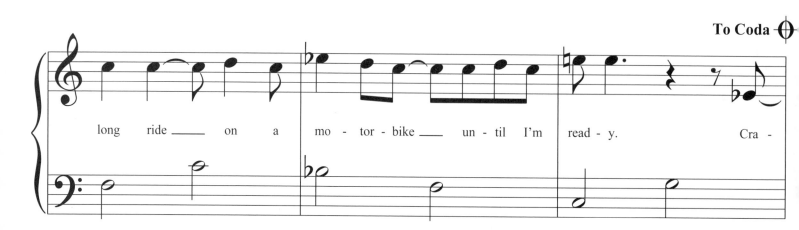

long ride __ on a mo - tor - bike __ un - til I'm read - y. Cra -

- zy lit - tle thing called love.

D.S. al Coda

I got - ta be cool, __

CODA

- zy lit - tle thing called love.   This thing __

__ called love,   I __ just __ can't __

han - dle it. __ This   thing   called   love,   I __ must __

get a - round to it. ___ I ain't __ read - y. Cra -

- zy lit - tle thing called love, cra - zy lit - tle thing called

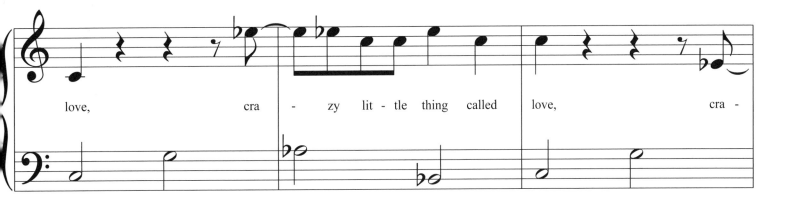

love, cra - zy lit - tle thing called love, cra -

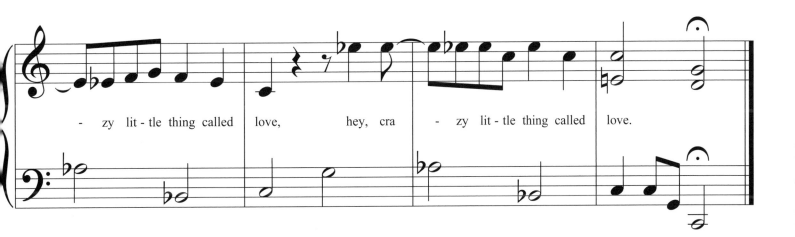

- zy lit - tle thing called love, hey, cra - zy lit - tle thing called love.

DOWNTON ABBEY
(Theme)

Music by JOHN LUNN

Moving along

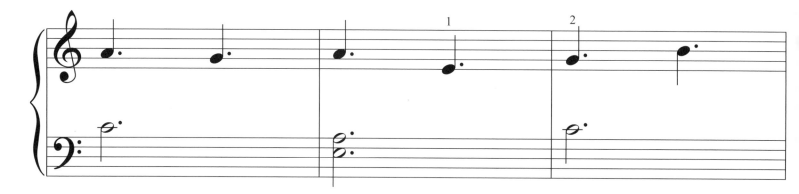

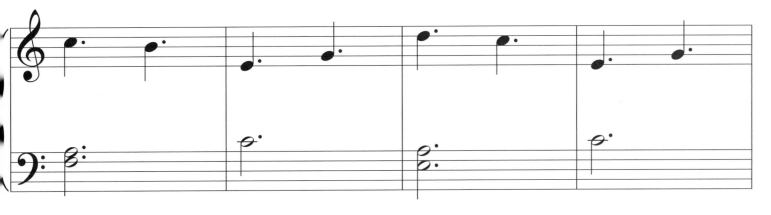

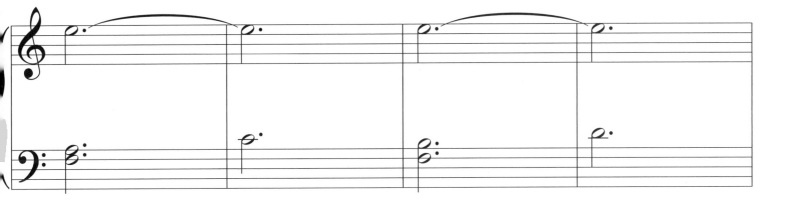

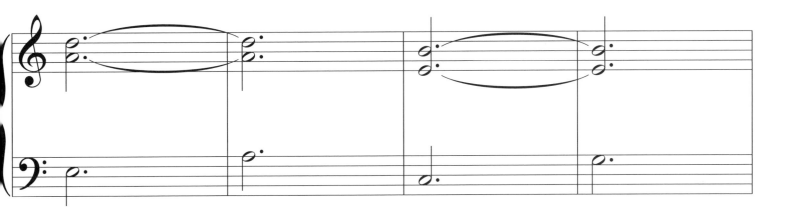

ELASTIGIRL IS BACK

from INCREDIBLES 2

Composed by MICHAEL GIACCHINO

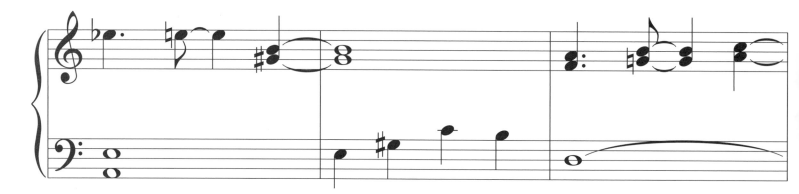

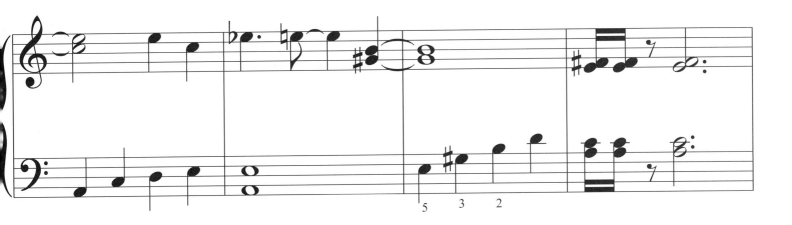

THE HIDDEN WORLD

from the Motion Picture HOW TO TRAIN YOUR DRAGON: THE HIDDEN WORLD

By JOHN POWELL

Slowly

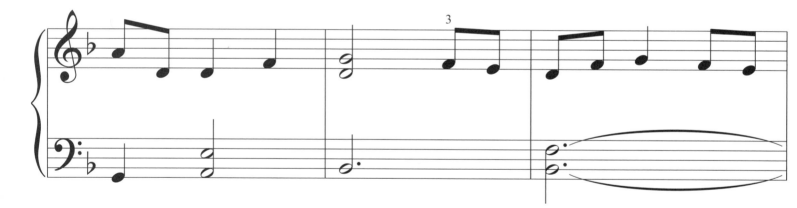

Broaden

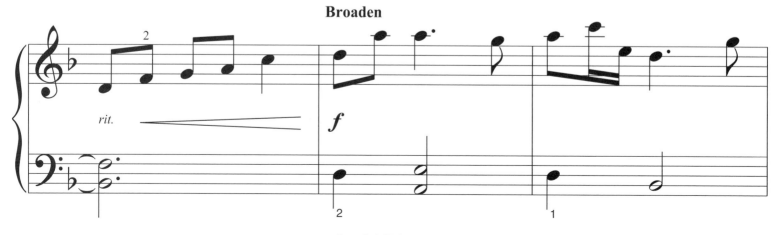

A MILLION DREAMS

from THE GREATEST SHOWMAN

Words and Music by BENJ PASEK
and JUSTIN PAUL

Moderately, with intensity

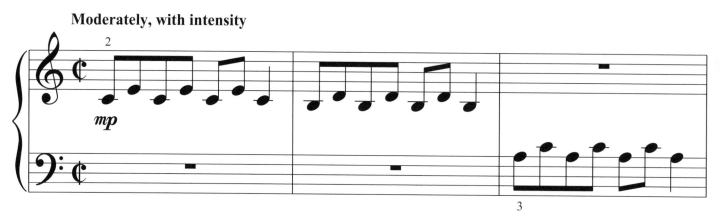

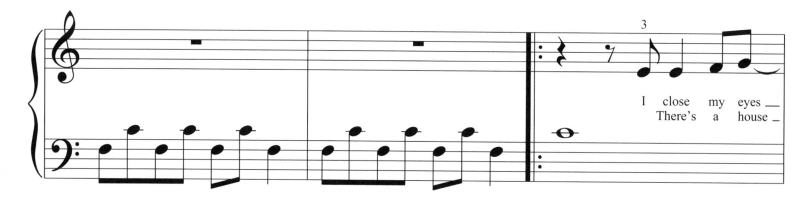

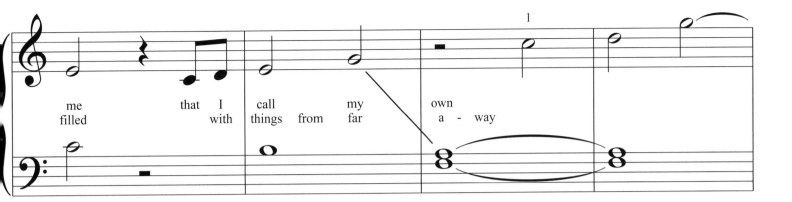

me
filled
that I
with
call
things from
my
far
own
a - way

Through the dark, _____ through the door, _____ through where no _____
Spe - cial things _____ I com - pile, _____ each one there _____

_____ one's been be - fore, but it feels like home
_____ to make you smile on a rain - y day

They can say, they can say it all _____ sounds cra - zy
They can say, they can say it all _____ sounds cra - zy

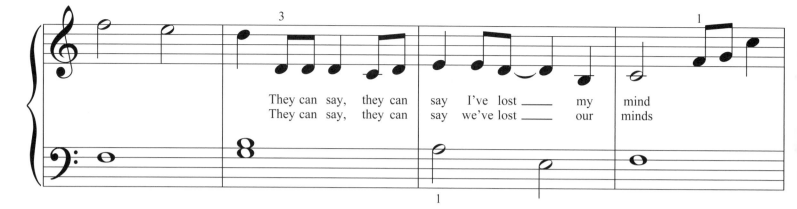

They can say, they can say I've lost ____ my mind
They can say, they can say we've lost ____ our minds

I don't care, I don't care, so call me cra - zy
I don't care, I don't care if they call us cra - zy

We can live in a world that we de - sign
Run a - way to a world that we de - sign

'Cause ev - 'ry night ____ I lie in bed the

bright - est col - ors   fill my head   A mil - lion dreams __ are

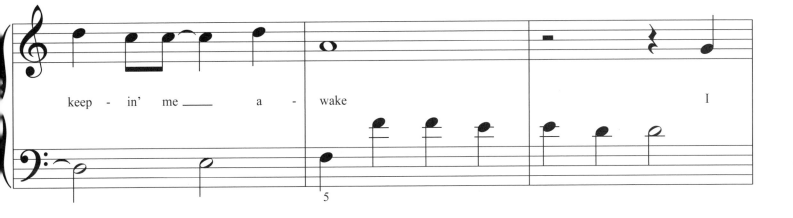

keep - in' me ____ a - wake   I

think of what ___ the   world could be,   a vi - sion of the

one I see   A mil - lion dreams ___ is   all it's gon - na take ___

Oh, a mil - lion dreams __ for the

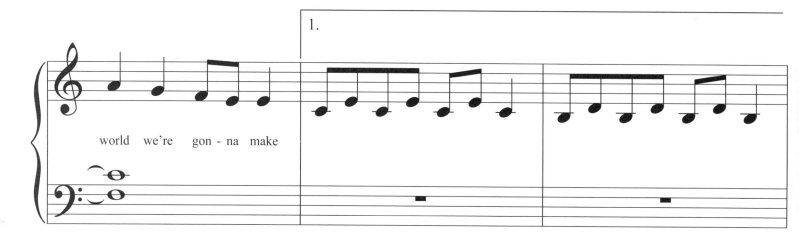

1.

world we're gon - na make

2.

How - ev - er

big, how - ev - er small, let me be part of it all __

Share your dreams ____ with me ____

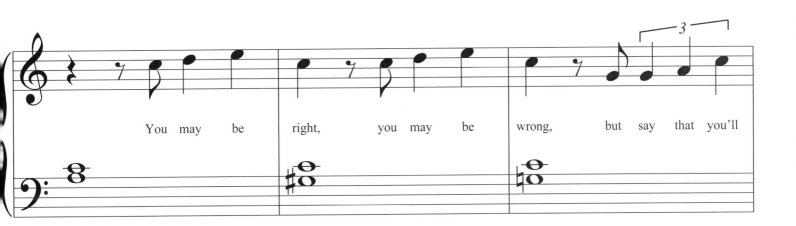

You may be right, you may be wrong, but say that you'll

bring me a-long ____ to the world you see, ____ To the

world I close my eyes to see, I close my eyes to

see _____ 'Cause ev - 'ry night ___ I lie in bed the

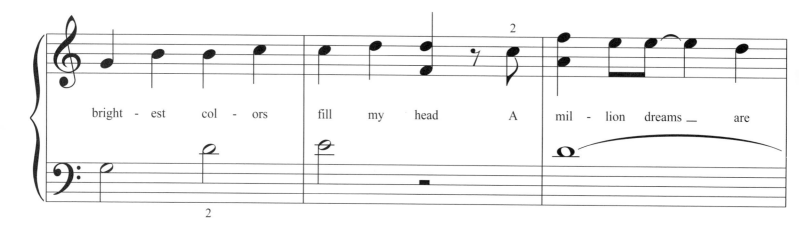

bright - est col - ors fill my head A mil - lion dreams ___ are

keep - in' me a - wake ___ A mil - lion dreams, ___ a mil - lion dreams ___ I

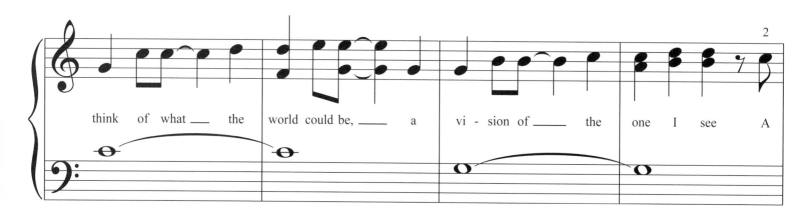

think of what ___ the world could be, ___ a vi - sion of ___ the one I see A

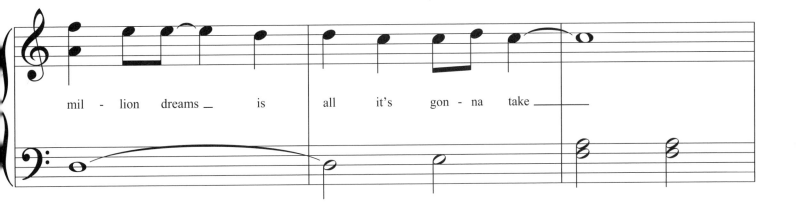

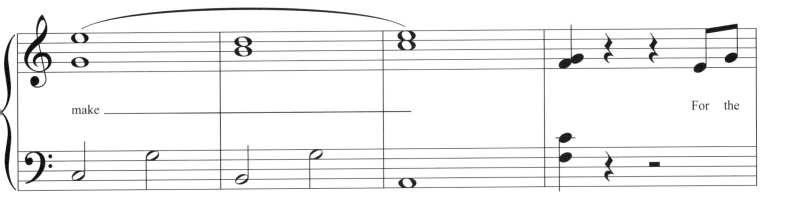

THE PLACE WHERE LOST THINGS GO

from MARY POPPINS RETURNS

Music by MARC SHAIMAN
Lyrics by SCOTT WITTMAN
and MARC SHAIMAN

Moderately

Do you ev- er lie a - wake at night,

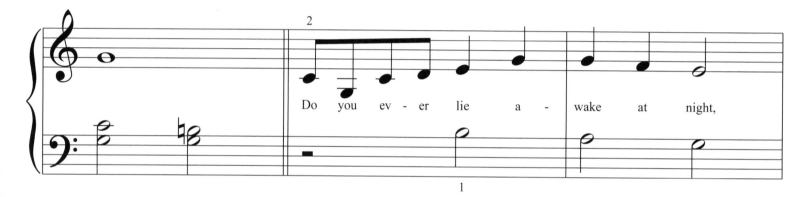

just be- tween the dark and the morn- ing light, search- ing for the things you

used to know, look- ing for the place where the lost things go?

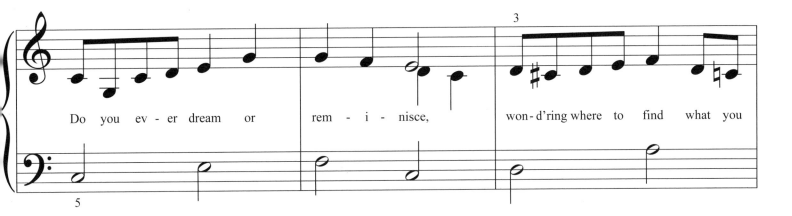

dis - ap - peared. Noth-ing's real - ly left, or lost with - out a trace.
lost is found. May - be on the moon, or may - be some-where new,

Noth-ing's gone for - ev - er, on - ly out of place. So, may - be now the dish and
may - be all you're miss - ing lives in - side of you. So, when you need her touch and

my best spoon are play - ing hide and seek just be - hind the moon,
lov - ing gaze, "gone, but not for - got - ten," is the per - fect phrase.

wait - ing there un - til it's time to show. Spring is like that now,
Smil - ing from a star that she makes glow, trust she's al - ways there,

far   be - neath   the   snow,
watch - ing   as   you   grow.

hid - ing   in   the   place   where   the
Find   her   in   the   place   where   the

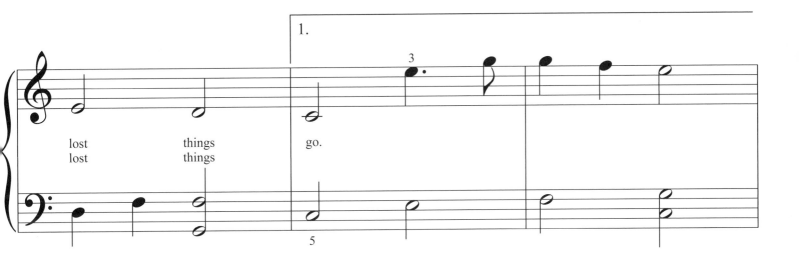

lost   things   go.
lost   things

go.

PROUD CORAZÓN
from COCO

Music by GERMAINE FRANCO
Lyrics by ADRIAN MOLINA

Moderately

Say that I'm cra - zy or

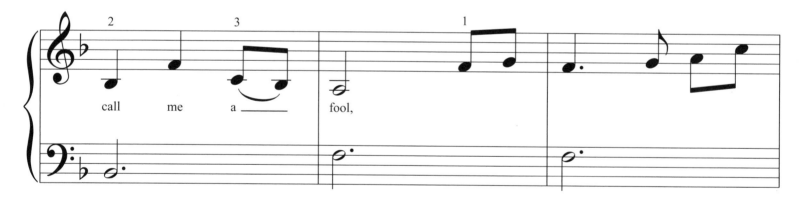

call me a _____ fool,

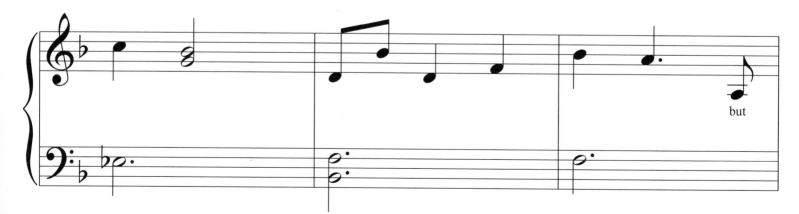

but

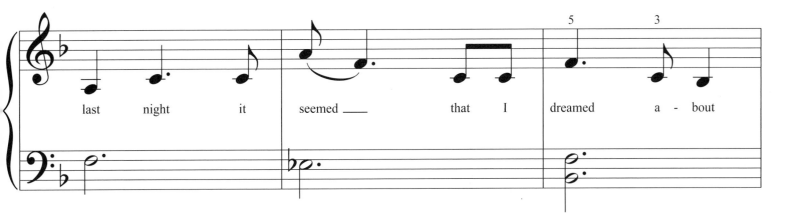

last night it seemed ___ that I dreamed a - bout

you.

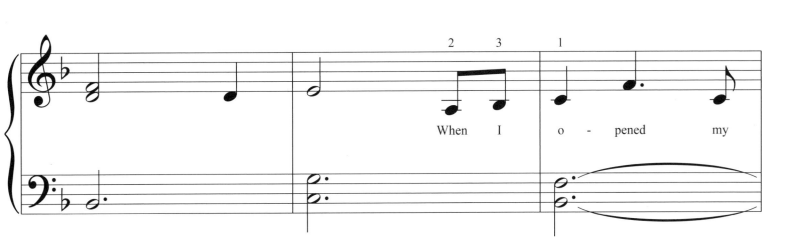

When I o - pened my

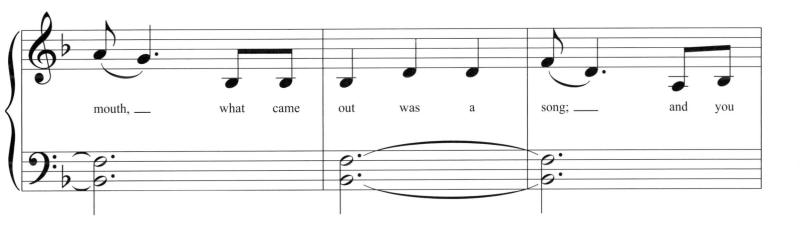

mouth, ___ what came out was a song; ___ and you

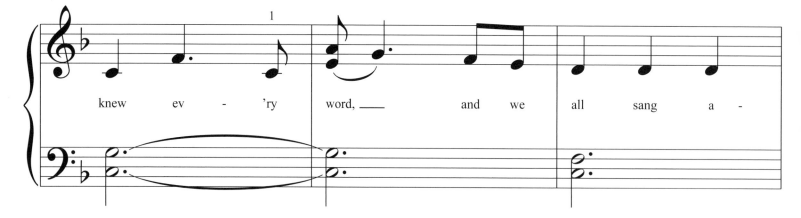

knew ev - 'ry word, ___ and we all sang a -

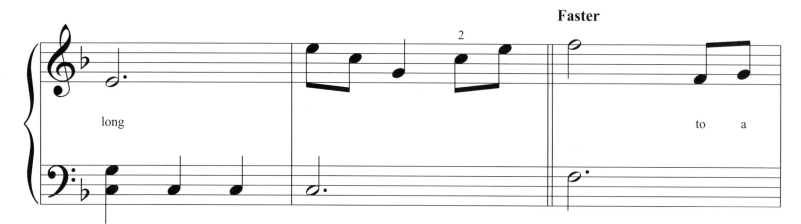

long to a

mel - o - dy played ___ on the strings of our

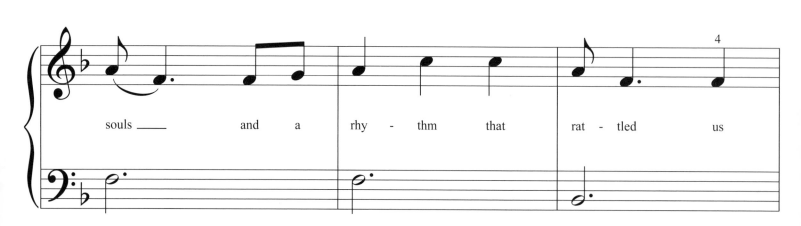

souls ___ and a rhy - thm that rat - tled us

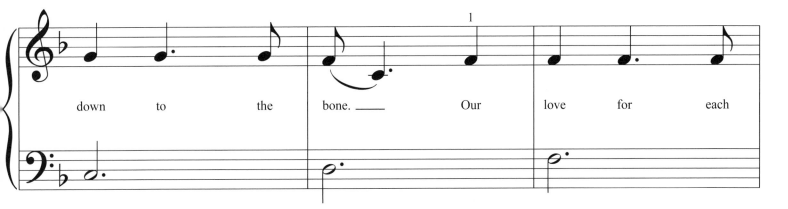

down to the bone. ____ Our love for each

oth - er will live on for - ev - er

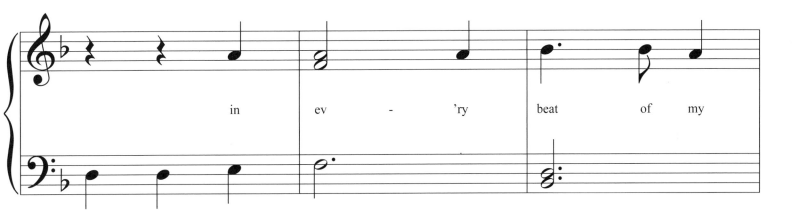

in ev - 'ry beat of my

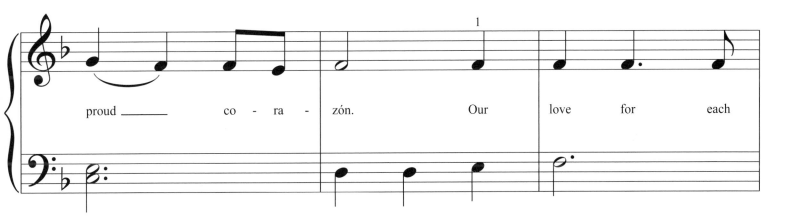

proud ____ co - ra - zón. Our love for each

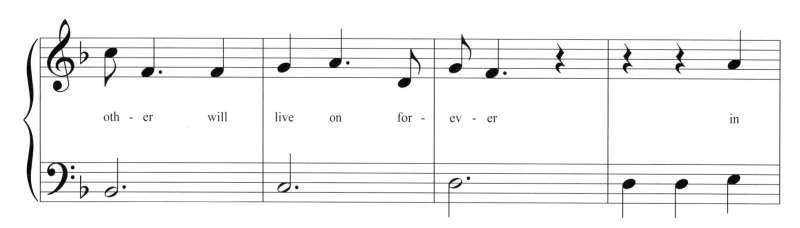

oth - er will live on for - ev - er in

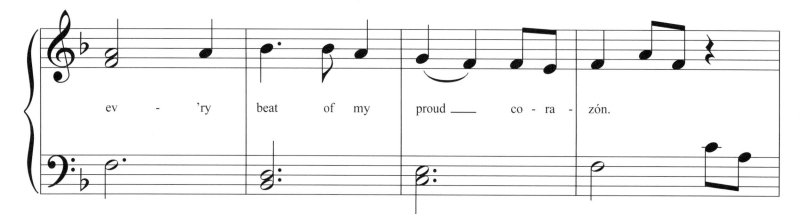

ev - 'ry beat of my proud ____ co - ra - zón.

Moderately, in 1

cresc. ¡Ay! Mi fa - *f*

mi - lia, oi - ga mi gen - te. Can - ten a

co - ro. _____ Let it be known: _____ Our love for each

oth - er will live on for - ev - er in ev - 'ry

1.
beat of my proud _____ co - ra - zón.

2.
proud _____ co - ra -

zón.

SHALLOW

from A STAR IS BORN

Words and Music by STEFANI GERMANOTTA,
MARK RONSON, ANDREW WYATT
and ANTHONY ROSSOMANDO

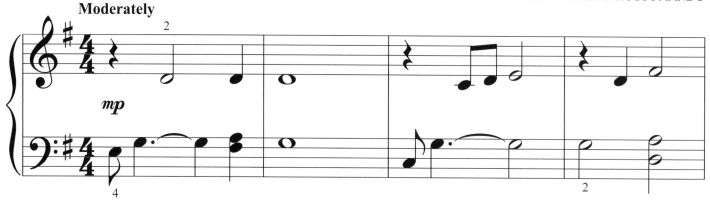

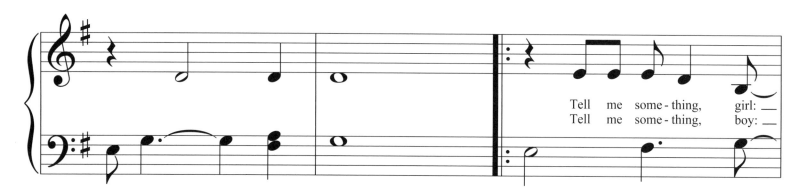

Tell me some-thing, girl: ___
Tell me some-thing, boy: ___

are you hap-py in this mod-ern world, ___
aren't you tired, ___ tryin' to fill that void, ___

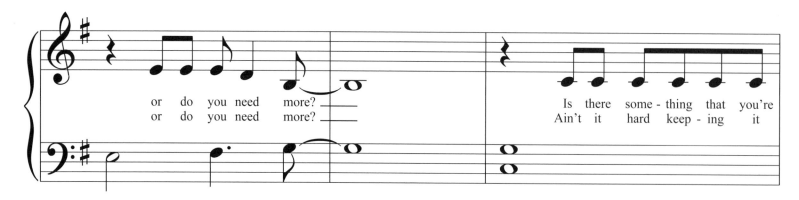

or do you need more? ___
or do you need more? ___

Is there some-thing that you're
Ain't it hard keep-ing it

search - ing for? _____
so hard - core? _____
I'm fall - ing.

In all the good times I find my - self ____ long - ing ____ for

change, and in the bad times I fear my - self.

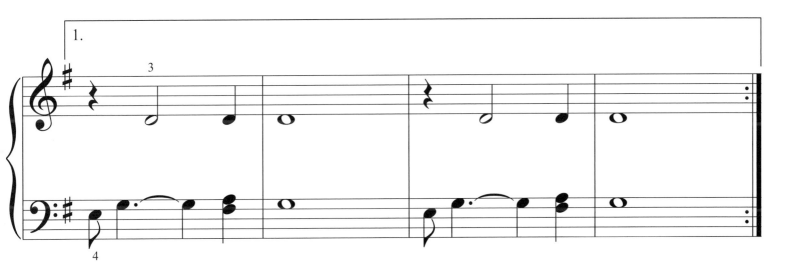

1.

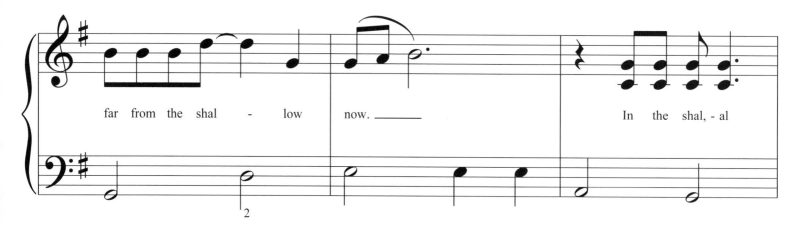

In the shal, -al, - shal, -al - low, ____ we're far from the shal - low

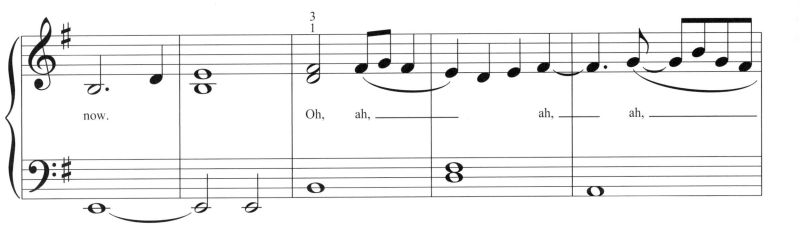

now.   Oh,   ah, ____   ah, ____   ah, ____

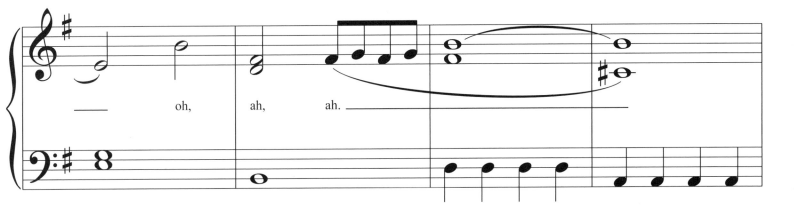

____   oh,   ah,   ah. ____

I'm off the deep ___ end.   Watch as I dive ___ in: I'll nev - er meet ___ the

ground. ___ Crash through the sur - face, where they can't hurt ___ us. We're

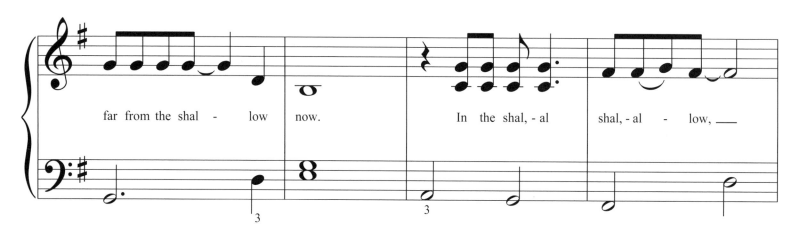

far from the shal - low now. In the shal, - al shal, - al - low, ___

in the shal, shal, - al, - al, - al, - low. ___ In the shal, - al, -

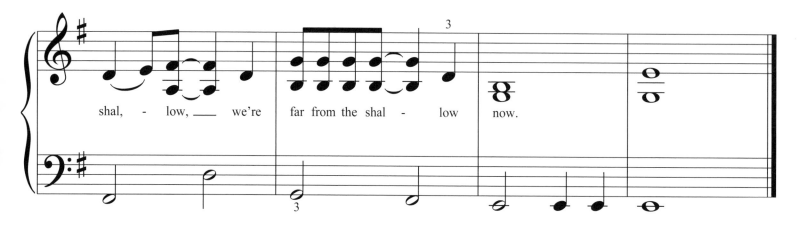

shal, - low, ___ we're far from the shal - low now.

ZERO
from RALPH BREAKS THE INTERNET

Words and Music by DAN REYNOLDS,
WAYNE SERMON, BEN McKEE,
DANIEL PLATZMAN and JOHN HILL

With energy, in 2

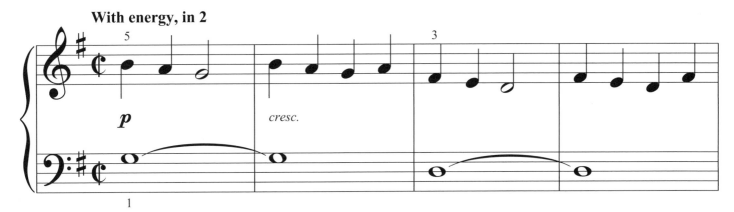

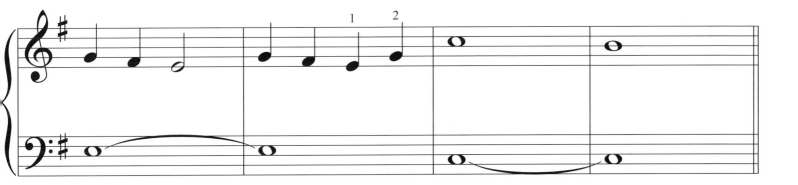

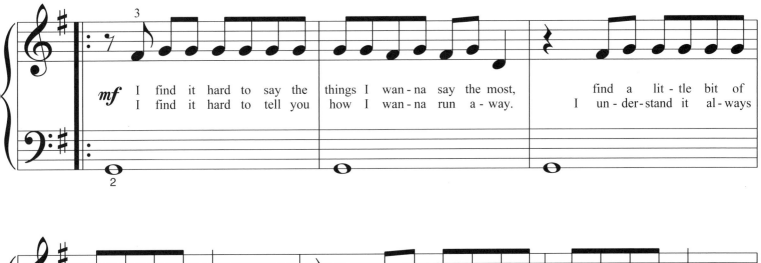

I find it hard to say the things I wan-na say the most, find a lit-tle bit of
I find it hard to tell you how I wan-na run a-way. I un-der-stand it al-ways

stead-y as I get close, find a bal-ance in the mid-dle of the cha-os.
makes you feel a cer-tain way. I find a bal-ance in the mid-dle of the cha-os.

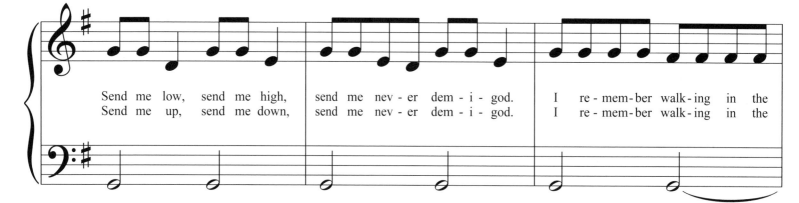

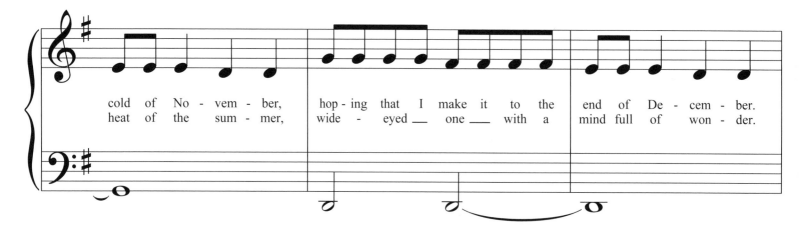

look-ing for the path of the young and lone-ly. I don't wan-na hear a-bout

what to do. ___ I don't wan-na do it just to do it for you.

Hel-lo, hel-lo. Let me tell you what it's like to be a ze-ro, ze-ro. Let me

show you what it's like to al-ways feel, ___ feel ___ like I'm emp-ty and there's noth-ing real-ly

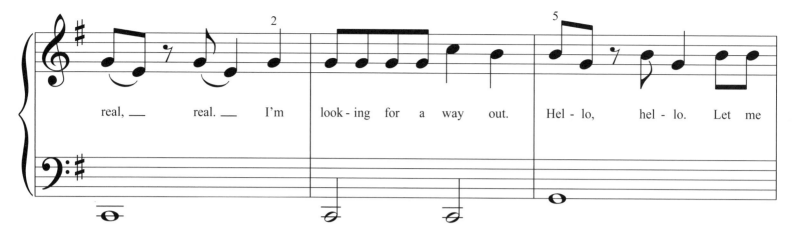

real, ___ real. ___ I'm look-ing for a way out. Hel - lo, hel - lo. Let me

tell you what it's like to be a ze - ro, ze - ro. Let me show you what it's like to nev - er

feel, ___ feel ___ like I'm good e - nough for an - y - thing that's real, ___ real. ___ I'm

To Coda ⊕   **Slower, with freedom**

look - ing for a way out.   Let me tell you 'bout
                                 Let me tell you 'bout

it,   let   me   tell   you 'bout   it.   May - be   you're   the   same   as
it,   let   me   tell   tell   you 'bout   it.   They   say   truth   will   set   as   you

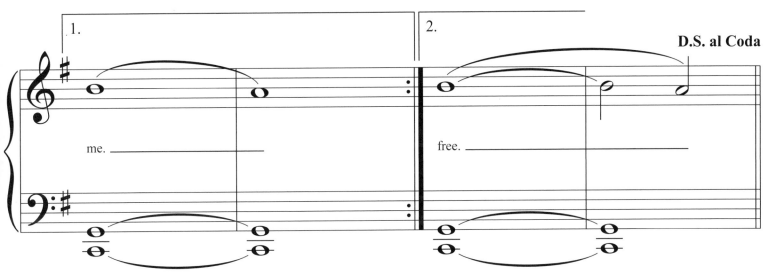

1.

me. _____

2.

D.S. al Coda

free. _____

CODA

f

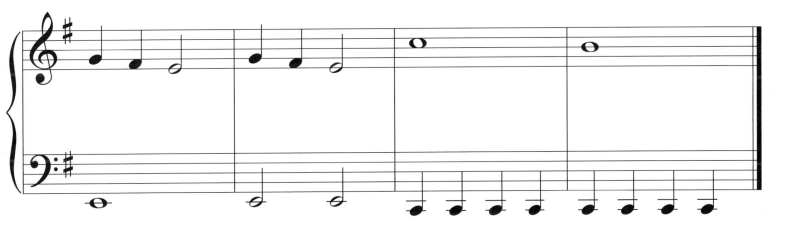

SPEECHLESS
from ALADDIN

Music by ALAN MENKEN
Lyrics by BENJ PASEK
and JUSTIN PAUL

Half-time feel

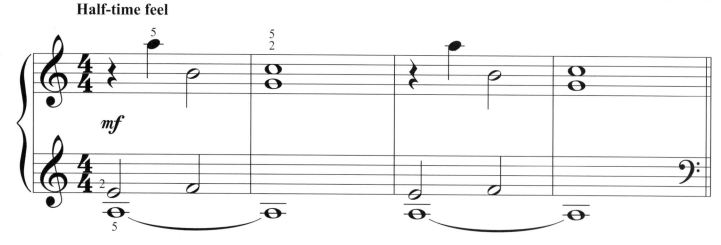

Here comes a wave __ meant to wash __ me a - way, a tide that is tak - ing me

un - der. Swal - low - ing sand, __ left with noth - ing to say, my

voice drowned out in the thun - der. But I won't cry, and

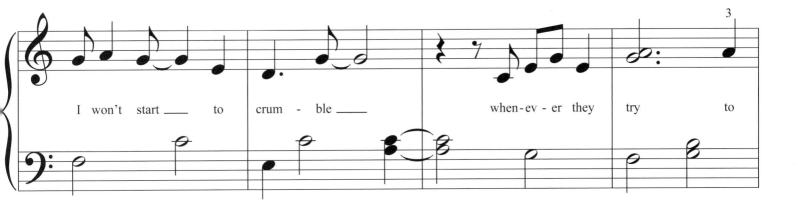

I won't start ___ to crum - ble ___ when-ev - er they try to

shut me or cut me ___ down. I won't be ___ si - lenced.

You can't keep me qui - et. Won't trem - ble when ___ you try it. All I know ___

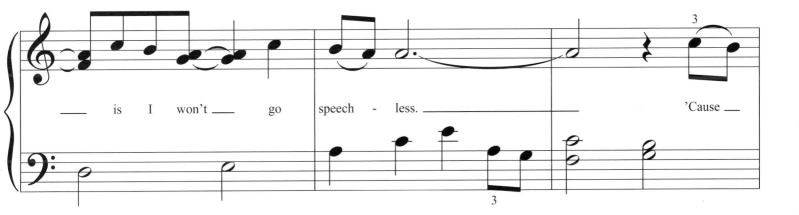

___ is I won't ___ go speech - less. ___ 'Cause ___

I'll   breathe   when   they   try   to   suf - fo - cate   me.   Don't   you

un - der - es - ti - mate   me,   'cause I know ____ that I won't ____ go

speech - less.   Writ - ten   in   stone, ___   ev - 'ry

rule, ev - 'ry   word,   cen - tur - ies old ___ and un - bend - ing.

Stay in your place, ___ bet - ter seen ___ and not heard; well, now that sto - ry is

end - ing. 'Cause I, can - not start ___ to

crum - ble. ___ So come on and try, try to shut ___

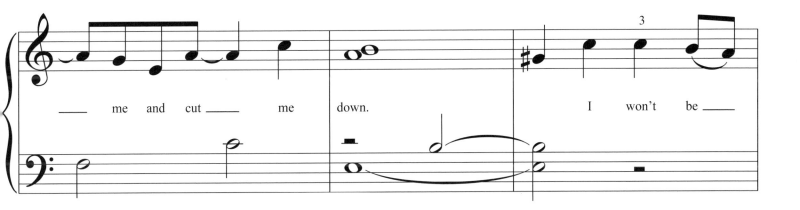

___ me and cut ___ me down. I won't be ___

si - lenced. You can't keep me qui - et. Won't

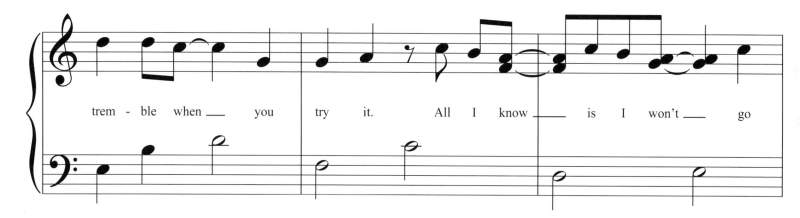

trem - ble when ___ you try it. All I know ___ is I won't ___ go

speech - less. Speech - less. ___ Let the storm in.

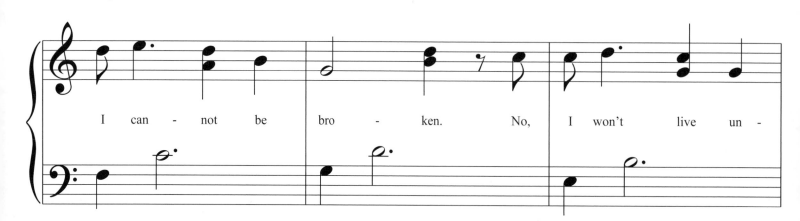

I can - not be bro - ken. No, I won't live un -

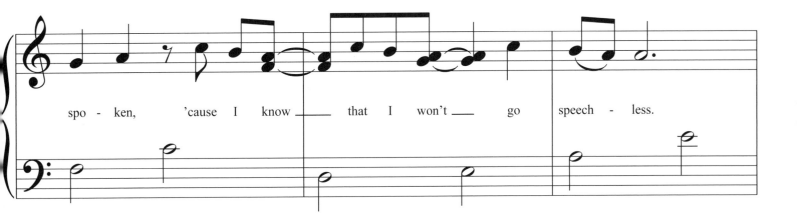

spo - ken, 'cause I know ____ that I won't ___ go speech - less.

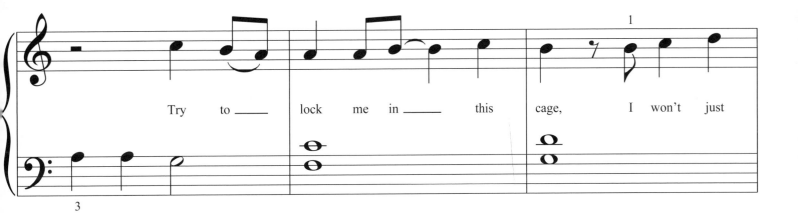

Try to ____ lock me in ____ this cage, I won't just

lay me down ___ and die. I will take these bro - ken

wings, and watch ___ me burn a - cross ___ the sky. Hear the

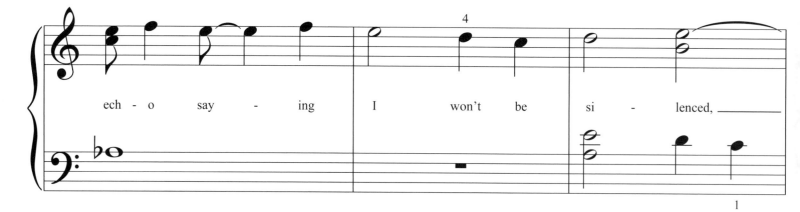

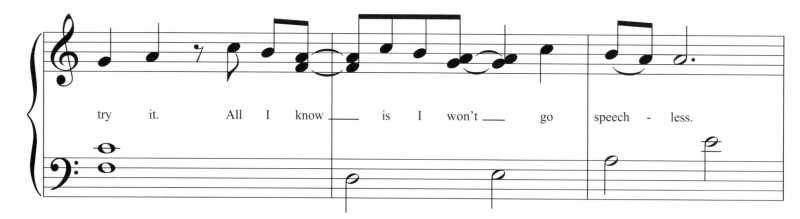

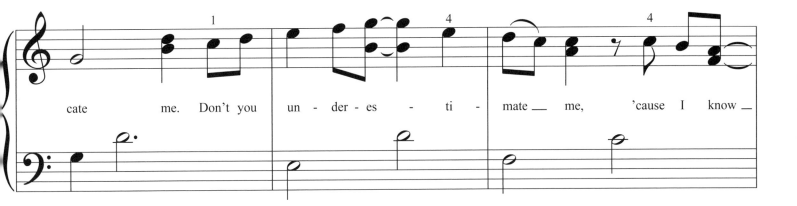

cate   me. Don't you   un - der - es - ti - mate ___ me,   'cause I   know ___

___ that   I won't ___ go   speech - less.   All I   know ___ ___   is   I won't ___   go

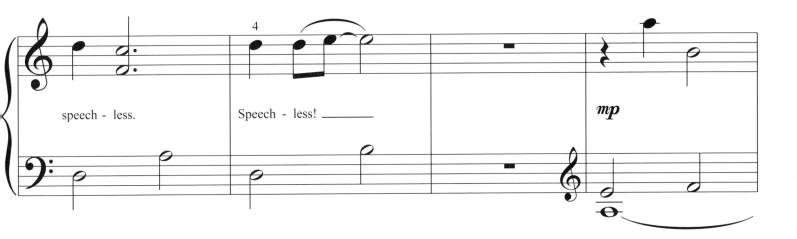

speech - less.   Speech - less! ___

WON'T YOU BE MY NEIGHBOR?

(It's a Beautiful Day in the Neighborhood)
featured in A BEAUTIFUL DAY IN THE NEIGHBORHOOD

Words and Music by
FRED ROGERS

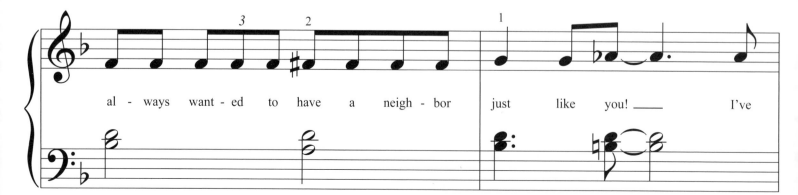

al - ways want - ed to live in a neigh - bor - hood with you, _____ so

let's make the most of this beau - ti - ful day. Since we're to - geth - er, we might as well say:

To Coda ⊕

Would you be mine? Could you be mine? Won't you be my neigh - bor? Won't you please, won't you please?

**D.C. al Coda
(with repeat)**

Please won't you be my neigh - bor?

CODA
⊕

Please won't you be my neigh - bor?

YESTERDAY

featured in YESTERDAY

Words and Music by JOHN LENNON
and PAUL McCARTNEY

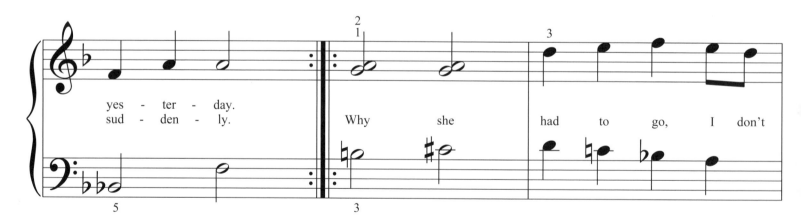

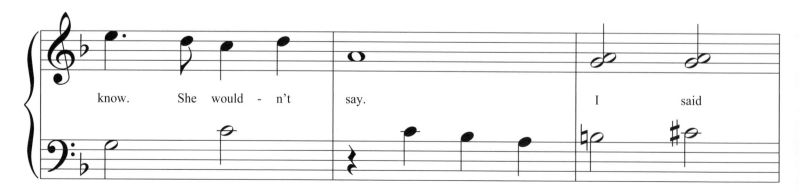

63

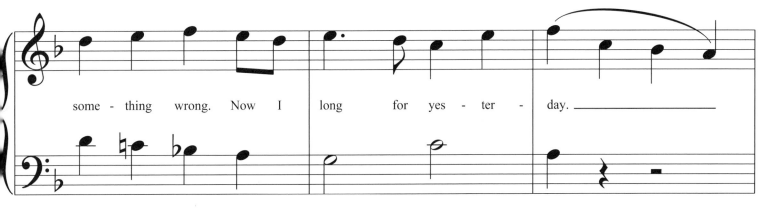

some - thing wrong. Now I long for yes - ter - day. _____

Yes - ter - day, love was such an eas - y game to play.

Now I need a place to hide a - way. Oh, I be - lieve in

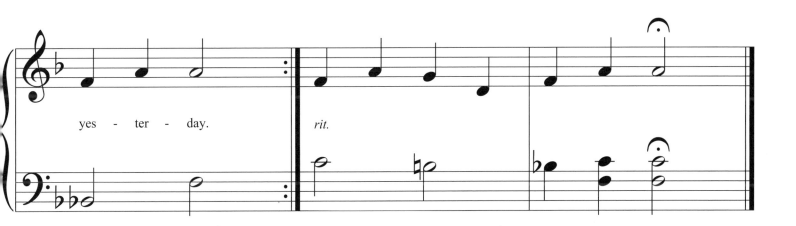

yes - ter - day. *rit.*

YOUR SONG
featured in ROCKETMAN

Words and Music by ELTON JOHN
and BERNIE TAUPIN

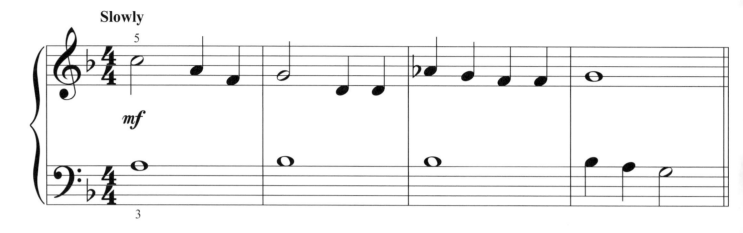

Slowly

mf

1.It's a lit - tle bit   fun - ny _____   this feel - ing in -   side. _____
2. If I was a   sculp - tor _____   but then _____ a - gain   no, _____ or a
4., 5. *(See additional lyrics)*

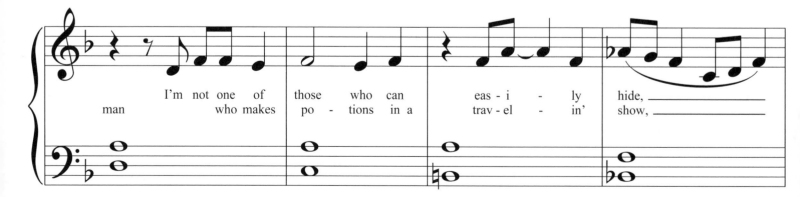

I'm not one of   those who can   eas - i - ly   hide, _____
man   who makes   po - tions in a   trav - el - in'   show, _____

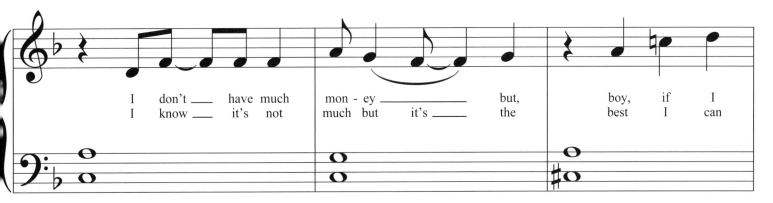

I don't ___ have much | mon-ey ___ but, | boy, if I
I know ___ it's not | much but it's ___ | the best I can

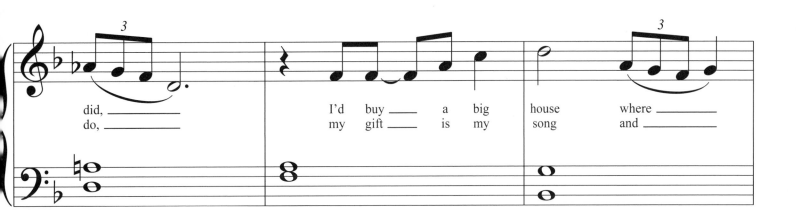

did, ___ | I'd buy ___ a big | house where ___
do, ___ | my gift ___ is my | song and ___

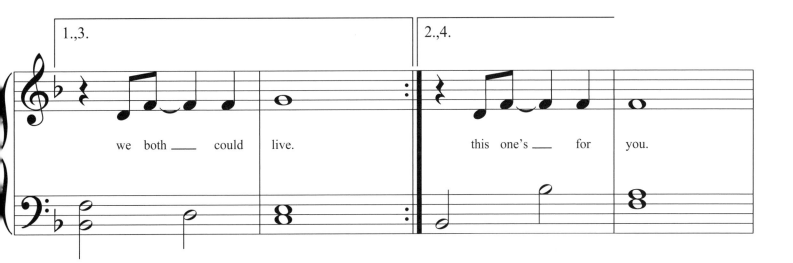

1.,3.

2.,4.

we both ___ could live. | this one's ___ for you.

3.,6. And you ___ can tell | ev - 'ry - bod - y | this is your | song. ___

To Coda ⊕

It may ___ be   quite ___ sim-ple but,   now that it's   done. ___

I hope you don't mind,   I hope you don't mind   that I put down in ___

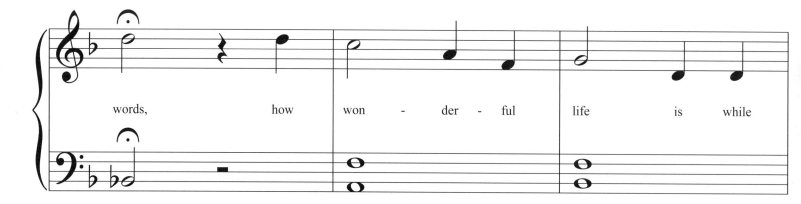

words,   how   won - der - ful   life   is   while

D.S. al Coda

you're ___ in the   world.

CODA

I hope you don't mind,   I hope you don't mind   that I put down in

1.

words,   how won - der - ful   life is while   you're in the

2.

world.   you're in the world.

Additional Lyrics

4. I sat on a roof and kicked off the moss.
Well, a few of the versions, well, they've got me quite cross.
But the sun's been quite kind while I wrote this song.
It's for people like you that keep it turned on.

5. So excuse me forgetting but these things I do.
You see I've forgotten if they're green or they're blue.
Anyway the thing is what I really mean,
Yours are the sweetest eyes I've ever seen.

SPIRIT
from Disney's THE LION KING 2019

Written by TIMOTHY McKENZIE,
ILYA SALMANZADEH and BEYONCÉ

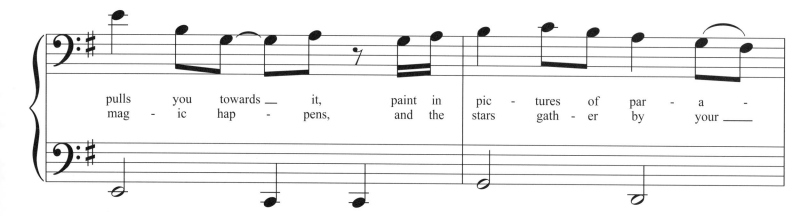

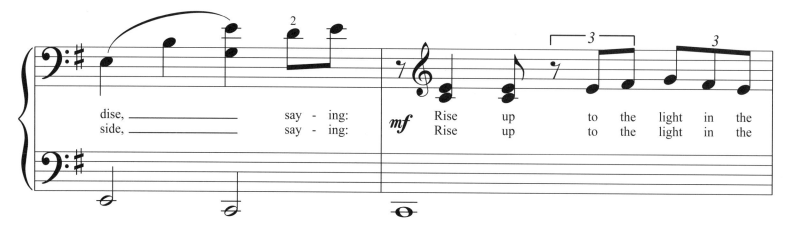

sky, yeah. Watch the light lift your
sky, yeah. Let the light lift your

heart up, burn your flame through the
heart up, burn your flame through the

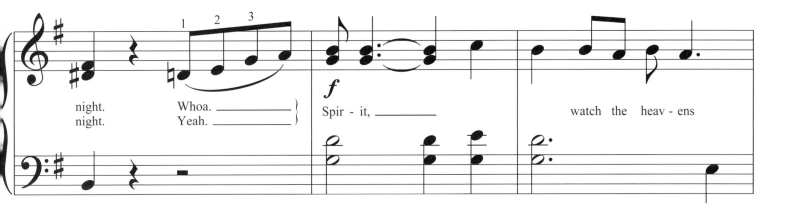

night. Whoa. _____
night. Yeah. _____

Spir - it, _____

watch the heav - ens

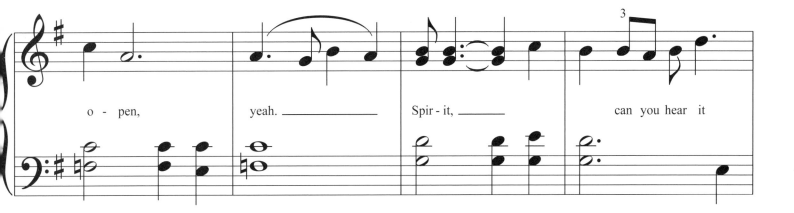

o - pen,

yeah. _____

Spir - it, _____

can you hear it

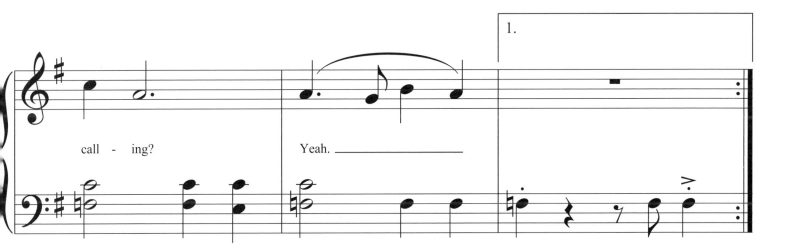

call - ing?

Yeah. _____

1.

70

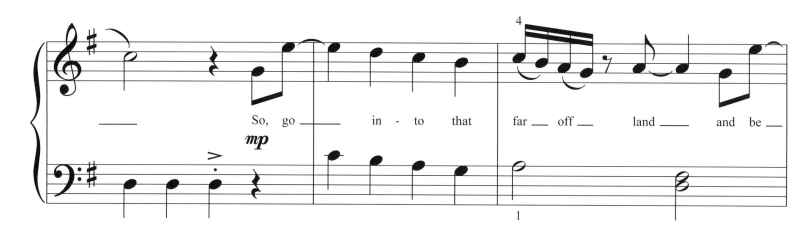

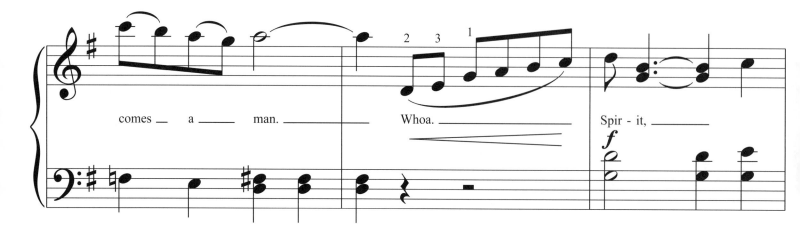

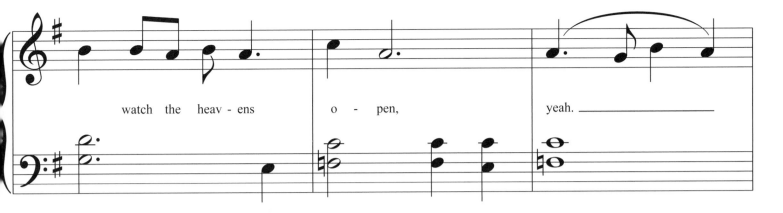

watch the heav - ens o - pen, yeah. _____

Spir - it, _____ can you hear it call - ing?

Yeah. _____ Spir - it, watch the heav - ens o - pen,

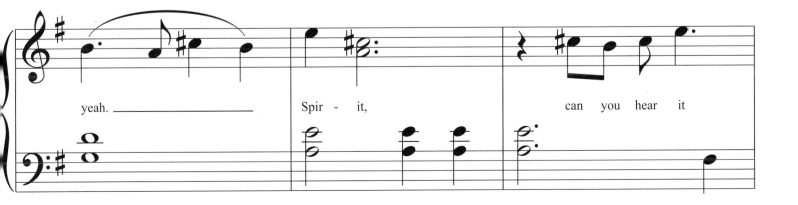

yeah. _____ Spir - it, can you hear it

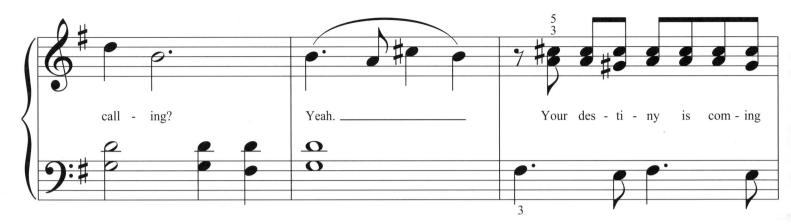

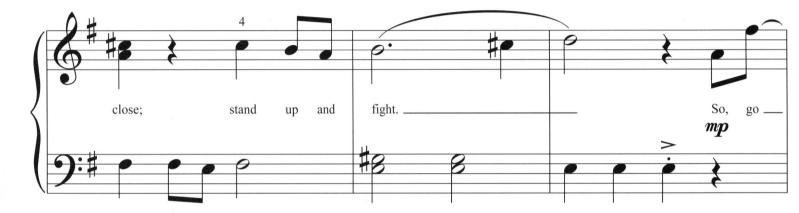

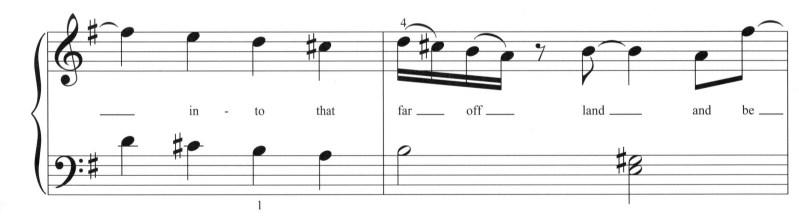